EDGE BOOKS

Truth and Rumors
SPORTS

by Sean Stewart Price   illustrations by Eldon Doty

Consultant:
Craig R. Coenen, PhD
Associate Professor of History
Mercer County Community College
West Windsor, New Jersey

CAPSTONE PRESS
a capstone imprint

J
796
PRICE

Edge Books are published by Capstone Press,
151 Good Counsel Drive, P.O. Box 669, Mankato, Minnesota 56002.
www.capstonepub.com

Copyright © 2011 by Capstone Press, a Capstone imprint.
All rights reserved.
No part of this publication may be reproduced in whole or in part,
or stored in a retrieval system, or transmitted in any form or by any means,
electronic, mechanical, photocopying, recording, or otherwise, without
written permission of the publisher.

RODGERS MEMORIAL LIBRARY
JAN 12 2017
$ 19.99

For information regarding permission, write to Capstone Press,
151 Good Counsel Drive, P.O. Box 669, Dept. R, Mankato, Minnesota 56002.
Printed in the United States of America North Mankato, Minnesota.
032010
005740CGF10

Books published by Capstone Press are manufactured with paper containing at least 10 percent post-consumer waste.

Library of Congress Cataloging-in-Publication Data
Price, Sean.
Sports : truth and rumors / by Sean Stewart Price.
p. cm.—(Edge Books. Truth and Rumors)
Includes bibliographical references and index.
Summary: "Labels common stories about sports as fact or fiction and teaches readers how to tell the difference between truth and rumors"—Provided by publisher.
ISBN 978-1-4296-4747-2 (library binding)
1. Sports—Juvenile literature. I. Title. II. Series.
GV705.4.P75 2011
796—dc22 2009054101

Editorial Credits

Aaron Sautter and Kathryn Clay, editors; Tracy Davies, designer; Marcie Spence, media researcher; Nathan Gassman, art director; Laura Manthe, production specialist

Photo Credits

AP Images/Pat Sullivan, cover (right)
Getty Images Inc./Don O'Reilly/Dozier Mobley, 13; Hulton Archive, 7; J.R. Eyerman/Time Life Pictures, 22; New York Times Co., 17; Photo File, 29 (bottom); Scott Levy, 14 (top); Spencer Arnold, 26 (top); Transcendental Graphics, 21
Library of Congress, 10 (both), 16
Newscom, cover (left), 8, 9, 25 (bottom), 28, 29 (top); Cliff Welch/Icon SMI, 26 (bottom); Kevin Sullivan/Orange County Register/MCT, 23; TSN/Icon SMI, 19; William C. Greene/TSN/Icon SMI, 20
Shutterstock/Carmen Ruiz, 6; Denis Babenko, cover (photo frame); Mr. B Hughes, 25 (top); Psycho, cover (brick wall); Tan Wei Ming, cover (ceramic tile); Tony Campbell, 14 (bottom)

Table of Contents

Sports: What's the Real Story?

Hello, sports fans! Over the years, there have been many great moments in sports. But are all sports stories real? Read the following stories and try to decide which one is true.

1. The lowest-scoring game in National Basketball Association (NBA) history took place on November 22, 1950. The Fort Wayne Pistons defeated the Minneapolis Lakers with a score of 19 to 18. Back then, teams didn't shoot the ball much. Instead they spent a lot of time fouling and shooting free throws. Fans grew bored with the low-scoring games. In 1954, the NBA began using a 24-second shot clock. The clock forced players to take more shots. Soon basketball became the fast-moving, high-scoring sport we know today.

2. On July 23, 1948, New York Yankees slugger Joe DiMaggio hit five foul balls. Three of them went past the left field foul line. The Yankees argued that the hits were fair and should have counted as home runs. At the time, there were no foul poles. Umpires couldn't easily tell if a ball was outside a line. DiMaggio's foul balls prompted Major League Baseball (MLB) to start using foul poles in the outfield.

Both stories could be true. But which one is? In sports, anything can happen. Athletes do amazing things all the time. They set new records. They make wild, incredible plays. Sometimes they have terrible games. And no matter how an athlete performs, fans often stretch the truth.

Read on to learn about some of the best-known myths and legends about sports. You'll also discover some strange-but-true stories that you can share with your friends.

Answers:
1. True; 2. False

Did ancient Greek athletes compete naked?

What's the story?

In the first Olympic games, the ancient Greek athletes competed totally naked. This shocked non-Greeks at the time. But the Greeks believed it was the best way to tell who was the best competitor.

CONSIDER THIS ...

Some people believe the ancient Greeks began competing naked after an accident. One Greek runner was wearing a loincloth during a race. The cloth fell off as he was running and caused him to trip. Other runners wanted to avoid the same fate. So they all took off their loincloths.

But competing naked could have begun for other reasons. The Greeks were big show-offs. Being naked helped others see who was most muscular and fit. Going naked also made them feel equal to one another. Only rich men could wear fine clothes. If everyone took off their clothes, no one knew who was rich or poor.

The VERDICT

Yes. Greeks trained and competed naked in most sports. However, they weren't always naked. In at least one ancient event, men had to run a race while wearing full battle armor.

FACT: The Greeks held competitions for just about everything. They even loved food-eating contests. People competed to see who could eat the most food in the shortest amount of time.

Is there a *Sports Illustrated* curse?

What's the story?

Sports Illustrated, or *SI*, is a top sports magazine in the United States. Athletes must perform extremely well to earn a spot on the magazine's cover. But something funny seems to happen to athletes who appear on the cover. They start performing poorly. Some say that appearing on the cover of *SI* curses an athlete's career.

THE EVIDENCE

In 2002, reporters for *SI* did a study on the curse. They found that about 37 percent of athletes had a decline in performance after appearing on the cover.

Why do some athletes seem to perform worse after appearing on an *SI* cover? Sports writers point out that most athletes appear on *SI* covers at the peak of their careers. Their performance naturally drops off after that point. No athlete is great forever.

The VERDICT

No. There is no real evidence of a curse. Some athletes even perform better after appearing on an *SI* cover. For example, basketball star Michael Jordan appeared on more than 50 covers. Yet he remained a great athlete throughout his career.

FACT: *Madden NFL* video games are very popular. But legend has it that football players who appear on the covers soon face nasty injuries that shorten their careers. Since 2001, almost everyone who has appeared on these covers has been injured or played poorly.

Billy Goat Curse

During the 1945 World Series, Chicago tavern owner Billy Sianis was asked to leave one of the games. His pet goat's smell bothered the Chicago Cubs fans at Wrigley Field. Sianis was angry and declared, "Them Cubs, they aren't gonna win no more." Some people believe the "Billy Goat Curse" means the Cubs won't win another World Series at Wrigley. So far, they haven't.

Was Jesse Owens snubbed by Adolf Hitler at the Olympics?

What's the story?

The 1936 Olympics were held in Berlin, Germany. German **dictator** Adolf Hitler planned to congratulate each winner. But when U.S. track star Jesse Owens won four gold medals, Hitler left the stadium. Hitler was angry that Owens, an African-American, beat white contestants.

NOT SO FAST . . .

On the first day of the Olympics, Hitler congratulated some of the winners. These winners were either Germans or Finns. But Hitler didn't shake hands with African-American high jumper Cornelius Johnson after his gold medal win.

Olympic officials wanted the athletes to be treated fairly. They asked Hitler to either shake hands with all the winners or none of them. Hitler chose none.

The VERDICT

No. Hitler didn't snub Owens personally. After the first day of competition, he refused to shake hands with any of the winners.

dictator—a person who has complete power to rule over a country

The Real Snub

In spite of his Olympic achievements, Owens was hardly acknowledged even in the United States. Most Olympic winners are invited to the White House. But President Franklin D. Roosevelt never invited Owens. In fact, Roosevelt never even sent a telegram to congratulate him on his medals. However, Owens did ride in a New York City parade in his honor.

Was NASCAR racing started by moonshiners?

What's the story?

In the 1920s, alcohol was illegal in the United States. Moonshiners made and sold illegal liquor. They drove super-fast cars to transport their liquor quickly. The cars also helped them outrun the police. Moonshiners soon began racing against one another for fun. These races paved the way for NASCAR racing.

CONSIDER THIS . . .

In 1947, the National Association for Stock Car Auto Racing, or NASCAR, was formed. At least one original NASCAR driver, Junior Johnson, was a real moonshiner.

Auto racing wasn't the only popular sport at the time. Since the early 1900s, horse racing had been popular across the country. People may have carried that tradition over to racing cars.

The VERDICT

No. Moonshiner races most likely helped inspire the creation of NASCAR. But most early racers had nothing to do with moonshining.

Junior Johnson

Was the Stanley Cup ever misplaced?

What's the story?

In 1924, the Montreal Canadiens won the National Hockey League (NHL) championship. The winning players put the Stanley Cup trophy in the trunk of one player's car. Later, they discovered the trophy was missing.

THE EVIDENCE . . .

The Stanley Cup is an unusual trophy. In other sports, the championship trophies are usually kept safe in special cases. However, Stanley Cup winners get a little more time with their trophy. Each player on the winning team gets to take it home for a day. As a result, the Cup has a very interesting history.

According to one story, a car carrying the Cup got a flat tire. The players took the trophy out of the trunk to get the spare tire. Afterward, they forgot the Stanley Cup in a snowbank.

The VERDICT

Yes. Montreal Canadiens players did leave the Stanley Cup sitting in a snowbank. Once they realized it was missing, some of the players drove back to where the car had broken down. They were happy to find the Cup just where they'd left it.

FACT: The original Stanley Cup was retired in 1969. A similar-looking silver bowl replaced the trophy. Each year, the winning players' names are etched onto the trophy. More levels are added over time. Today, the full Stanley Cup stands about 3 feet (0.9 meter) tall and weighs 36 pounds (16 kilograms).

Beating up the Stanley Cup

The Stanley Cup is probably the most abused trophy in all of sports. For a while in 1907, it was used as a flowerpot. In 1970, the trophy was stolen from the Hockey Hall of Fame but was later returned. It has also been lost by major airlines. In 1991 and 1993, players accidentally sank the Cup in their swimming pools. The Stanley Cup has even been used as a dog bowl!

Did a young boy ever say, "Say it ain't so, Joe"?

What's the story?

In 1919, the Chicago White Sox purposely lost the World Series. The star of the team was "Shoeless" Joe Jackson. One heartbroken young fan came up to Jackson and said, "Say it ain't so, Joe." The phrase has been famous ever since.

CONSIDER THIS . . .

It was proven that Jackson and seven other players took money to lose the World Series on purpose. The players all faced criminal charges after they were caught. One newspaper printed a story about a young boy who walked up to Jackson as he left court. "It ain't true, is it, Joe?" the boy asked.

"Yes, kid, I'm afraid it is," Jackson replied. Later reporters changed the boy's words to, "Say it ain't so, Joe."

The VERDICT

Maybe. Newspapers did report Jackson's conversation with the boy. But reporters liked to add drama to their stories. They may have made up quotations. Years later Jackson said that the story was a myth. But Jackson may have said this to help fix his **reputation**.

York Times.

WEDNESDAY, SEPTEMBER 29, 1920. TWO CENTS

EIGHT WHITE SOX PLAYERS ARE INDICTED ON CHARGE OF FIXING 1919 WORLD SERIES; CICOTTE GOT $10,000 AND JACKSON $5,000

Yankee Owners Give Praise to Comiskey And Offer Him Use of Their Whole Team

COMISKEY SUSPENDS THEM

Promises to Run Them Out of Baseball if

reputation—your character, as judged by other people

FACT: There is no doubt that the Sox lost the Series on purpose. But a Chicago court found them not guilty of fraud charges. Even so, Major League Baseball banned all eight players from baseball for life.

A Nickname is Born

Jackson's nickname came early in his career. One day a pair of new shoes blistered his feet. He found it too painful to wear any shoes at all. So Jackson played a game in his socks and hit a triple. As he ran for third base one fan yelled, "You shoeless son of a gun, you!" Jackson never went without shoes again. But the nickname "Shoeless" Joe stuck.

Did George Gipp really say, "Win one for the Gipper"?

What's the story?

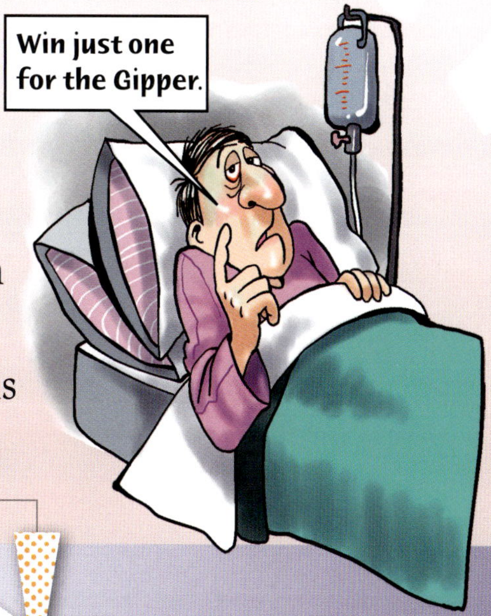

In the 1910s and 1920s, Notre Dame was a college football powerhouse under coach Knute Rockne. During one game in 1928, Rockne rallied his team by quoting a dying player named George Gipp. On his deathbed, Gipp told Rockne to "win just one for the Gipper."

CONSIDER THIS . . .

George Gipp had been one of Rockne's star players. But in 1920, he became sick and died at age 25. Eight years later, Notre Dame was playing Army. Army's powerful team outscored the Fighting Irish in the first half. Rockne inspired his team with a powerful halftime speech.

Rockne told his players about being at Gipp's deathbed. According to Rockne, some of Gipp's last words went like this: "I've got to go, Rock. It's all right. I'm not afraid. Sometime, Rock, when the team is up against it, when things are wrong and the breaks are beating the boys, ask them to go in there with all they've got and win just one for the Gipper."

The VERDICT

Maybe. Many historians doubt that Gipp made this speech to Rockne. Notre Dame was having a terrible season in 1928. Rockne was desperate to find a way to put some spirit into his team. But whether it's true or not, the speech worked. Notre Dame came from behind to beat Army 12–6.

Knute Rockne

Did Babe Ruth make a "called shot" home run?

What's the story?

Yankees slugger Babe Ruth came up to bat in Game 3 of the 1932 World Series. Ruth pointed to a spot beyond the center field fence. On the next pitch he hit a home run to that spot. Fans believed Ruth picked his shot and hit it exactly where he wanted it to go.

NOT SO FAST . . .

Ruth had already hit a homer earlier in the game. The next time Ruth came up to bat, Chicago Cubs fans booed him. Some people say Ruth got angry and started waving and pointing his arm. He might have been pointing at the pitcher or the Cubs dugout. Or he may have been pointing toward the stands. On the very next pitch, Ruth hit the ball over the center field stands. The next day, only one reporter declared that Ruth had made a "called shot." Yet the story was repeated over and over.

The VERDICT

Maybe. Pitcher Charlie Root swore that Ruth was not pointing to the outfield. Ruth's teammate Lou Gehrig was sure that he had. Ruth himself remained quiet on the subject. He let people make up their own minds. Even today, sports writers and baseball fans argue about Ruth's "called shot."

Babe Ruth's Home Run Promise

In 1926, Ruth supposedly visited a sick boy. Ruth promised the boy that he would hit a home run for him in the next game. Then he did just that. Is this story true? Mostly, but the story has changed over time.

Johnny Sylvester became gravely ill after being thrown from a horse. Ruth heard about Sylvester's story and sent the boy an autographed ball. It read, "I'll knock a homer for you in Wednesday's game." Then Ruth hit three home runs that day. Ruth didn't actually visit the boy until after the game.

Did the Globetrotters help create modern basketball?

What's the story?

In the 1940s and early 1950s, pro basketball games weren't very exciting. There were a lot of fouls and free throws but not much shooting. Basketball changed partly because of the Harlem Globetrotters. The Globetrotters used trick shots and fancy moves. Professional players began using some of the same moves.

THE EVIDENCE

The Globetrotters formed in 1929. The African-American team clowned around on the court and made people laugh.

In the early 1950s, Globetrotter shows were more popular than NBA games. But then the NBA began accepting African-American players. Some of the Globetrotters left to play in the NBA. NBA players also began using some of the Globetrotters' moves. The formerly slow game became flashy and fast-paced.

The VERDICT

Yes. The Globetrotters helped make pro basketball more exciting. Professional players began making fancy passes and slam dunks. This new, freewheeling style made basketball much more popular.

FACT: On March 2, 1962, former Globetrotter Wilt Chamberlain became the first NBA player to score 100 points in a single game. No other NBA player has accomplished this feat.

Do sewers back up during the Super Bowl?

What's the story?

Millions of people watch the Super Bowl every year. During the commercials, many of these viewers go to the bathroom at the same time. This overloads sewer systems and causes sewers to back up.

WAIT A SECOND . . .

In 1984, a large water pipe broke in Salt Lake City during the Super Bowl. People said it was because too many toilets were flushed at once. However, there was no tie between the broken water pipe and toilet use.

Similar stories have been told for years. During the 1930s, people said the same thing happened during popular radio shows.

The VERDICT

No. People don't go to the bathroom only during the Super Bowl commercials. They go all the time. Toilet use during the commercials does rise during Super Bowls. But it never threatens to flood any sewer system.

The Disney World Legend—Exposed!

According to one myth, Disney World has few visitors on Super Bowl Sunday. Park attendance does go down in the winter months. The cooler weather keeps many tourists away. But attendance on Super Bowl Sunday is about the same as any other Sunday in January and February. Some people seem to be fine with missing the Super Bowl—as long as they get to see Mickey and Minnie Mouse.

Does "golf" stand for Gentlemen Only, Ladies Forbidden?

What's the story?

Golf started off as a men's game. Women were not allowed to play. In fact, the word "golf" started out as an **acronym**. It stands for Gentlemen Only, Ladies Forbidden.

THE EVIDENCE . . .

The modern game of golf started in the 1550s in Scotland. In the past, golf was strictly for men. That tradition remains true in several places today. For example, the Augusta National Golf Club remains a male-only club.

The VERDICT

No. There are several ideas about how the word "golf" got started. But it did not start off as an acronym. Acronyms were uncommon before the 1900s. Also, the word was originally spelled several different ways. These included goulf, gouff, goiff, and golph.

acronym—a word made from the first or first few letters of the words in a phrase

FACT OR FICTION?:
How to Tell the Difference

Athletes often get caught up in scandals and rumors. These matters usually have little or nothing to do with their performance. But they can reflect on the athlete's character and reputation. They can also have a deep impact on the athlete's life. The following stories all affected players' lives in a major way. Can you tell which of the stories are true?

1. **Little League player Danny Almonte pitched a perfect game in 2001. With Danny's help, the Rolando Paulino All-Stars team made it to the Little League World Series. But shortly after their third-place finish, the team was disqualified. Officials found out that Danny was too old to compete. Danny's father had lied about his son's age, telling coaches he was only 12 years old. Danny was really 14.**

2. In 1967, Muhammad Ali was banned from boxing for refusing to join the U.S. Army. At the time, the United States was fighting the Vietnam War (1959–1975). Ali objected to the war and refused to fight in it. At the time, the country drafted young men into the army. Ali refused to be drafted, a crime punishable by prison time. Ali never went to prison. But the heavyweight champion was stripped of his title and banned from boxing for three years.

3. In 1985, Pete Rose set baseball's all-time hit record. He also played in six World Series. Rose seemed sure to become a member of the Baseball Hall of Fame. However, in 1989 Rose was caught betting on baseball games. This was against the rules for MLB players and managers. Rose was banned from baseball for life and was not admitted to the Hall of Fame.

Which of these stories is true? They all are! To sort out the truth from rumors, do research to get the whole story. Use the Internet to find experts at museums, history centers, and universities. Make phone calls and ask questions. Books, magazines, and newspapers can be very valuable resources. Ask a librarian if you cannot tell if a source is reliable. Do your research and you'll have no problem figuring out the difference between rumors and facts.

Glossary

acronym (AK-ruh-nim)—a word made from the first or first few letters of the words in a phrase; NBA is an acronym for National Basketball Association

dictator (DIK-tay-tuhr)—a person who has complete power to rule over a country

evidence (EV-uh-duhnss)—information, items, and facts that help prove something is true or false

fiction (FIK-shuhn)—a story about characters or events that are not real

loincloth (LOIN-klawth)—a piece of clothing worn around the waist and between the legs

reputation (rep-yuh-TAY-shuhn)—your character, as judged by other people

scandal (SKAN-duhl)—a dishonest or immoral act that shocks and embarrasses those involved

Read More

Berman, Len. *The Greatest Moments in Sports.* Naperville, Ill.: Sourcebooks, 2009.

Platt, Richard. *They Played What?! : The Weird History of Sports and Recreation.* Minnetonka, Minn.: Two-Can, 2007.

Porterfield, Jason. *Major League Baseball: The Great Steroid Scandals.* Disgraced! The Dirty History of Performance-Enhancing Drugs in Sports. New York: Rosen Central, 2010.

Internet Sites

FactHound offers a safe, fun way to find Internet sites related to this book. All of the sites on FactHound have been researched by our staff.

Here's all you do:

Visit *www.facthound.com*

FactHound will fetch the best sites for you!

Index

GEORGE H. & ELLA M.
RODGERS MEMORIAL LIBRARY
194 DERRY ROAD
HUDSON, NH 03051
WITHDRAWN

D1830076